MW01069223

Learning Through Entertainment, Inc.
wishes to thank the following
for their talent and participation in the creation of this book:
HarmonyGraphics
Audrey S. Johnston
Nicole Rothe
Michael Waker

ISBN 1-883681-06-5

Library of Congress 96-094136

Printed in the U.S.A.

First Printing, 1996

For The Parents...

The primary intention of this book is to offer gentle encouragement and training to the child who has recently reached potty training age. It's delightful rhymes and songs offer simple, pleasing directions to the child.

Here are some helpful hints to maximize the usefulness of this book.

1. Use a potty chair. It's size encourages children to use it by themselves. Plus, there is no fear of falling and no frightening pool of water.

2. Try switching to training pants. The fact that an "accident" is uncomfortable may add motivation for your child.

3. Dress your child in simple clothes that they can remove by themselves.

4. Help your child memorize these songs and rhymes through simple repetition— a key to achieving desirable behavior.

5. Encourage your child to take this book to the bathroom with them, as portrayed in the book itself. Make toilet training a calm, everyday function.

6. When your child uses the potty correctly, offer plenty of praise.

7. For those children who know what to do and when, but continue to have "accidents," you might allow them to help wash out their training pants.

In no time at all, your child will be an official member of the
Super Duper Pooper Club!

It's Potty Time.™

ILLUSTRATED BY

ROSE LYNN IMBLEAU

FOR

LEARNING™
Through Entertainment, Inc.

Hi, Kids!

My name is Mr. Penders.

I have a friend named

Today is a SPECIAL DAY for him.

BOBBY

Today is BOBBY'S BIRTHDAY,

and YOU'RE invited to his party!

Bobby is helping his Dad finish the
decorations. His mom is helping
sister Katy get ready for the party.

How about singing this birthday song for him?
OK Kids? Let's begin…

Today is Bobby's birthday, now he is four,
He is growing up now, more and more.
    He can dress himself,
    He can comb his hair.
He can throw a ball high into the air.

This is Bobby's birthday, we'll have a cake.
It's a cake that Bobby helped me make.
    From a box of candles,
    we counted out four,
Each year, Bobby learns more numbers than before.

Now Bobby knows animals by their names,
And he loves to play a hide-and-seek game.
    He can ride a trike,
    He can sing a song.
And he's old enough to stay up all day long.

This is Bobby's birthday, and he is four,
and he just keeps learning more and more.

"Come on Katy, let's go to the potty before Bobby's party begins," said Mom.

"Oh Katy, what's wrong? It's OK if you don't need to go right now. Just let me know when you *do* need to go," reassured Mom.

"Now why don't we sing the Potty Song…"

I can keep my panties dry
If I really, really try.
And I use my new potty
When I have to
poop and pee.

Bobby's friend
Lizzie is getting
ready to go to
his party too.

"Lizzie," said her Dad, "before we leave for Bobby's party, you need to go to the potty!"

"OK Daddy," said Lizzie.

"You need any help?" asked her Dad.

"No thanks, I can do it all by myself," replied Lizzie.

"That's my girl!" he said.

"First I'll get my book, then we'll both go to the potty," she said to her Teddy bear.

"When I use my potty, daddy's so proud of me."

As Lizzie and Teddy sit on their potties, Lizzie says:
"We're really good at this, aren't we, Teddy? Won't you sing one of my favorite songs with me?"

TO THE TUNE OF
ON TOP OF OLD SMOKEY...

On top of your potty,
    You're sitting to poop.
Oh life is much better,
    When your diapers don't droop.
But you have to be patient,
    Just sit there and smile.
        But instead of waiting…

Why not read for a while.

In no time at all, Lizzie and Teddy had finished.
"I'm done Daddy," said Lizzie.
"OK, don't forget to wipe, flush and wash your hands,"
said Lizzie's Dad.
"Now we have to wipe ourselves, Teddy. I'll show you how."

11

"There," said Lizzie. That's easy, isn't it? Here's a song to help you remember the right way to do it."

SUNG TO THE TUNE OF *ROW, ROW, ROW YOUR BOAT*

Wipe, wipe, wipe yourself, always front to back,
Care-fully, care-fully, now you have the knack.

"Now we have to flush and wash our hands, then we'll be all ready for Bobby's Party. I'll bet Daddy will be proud of both of us."

12

Lizzie sings

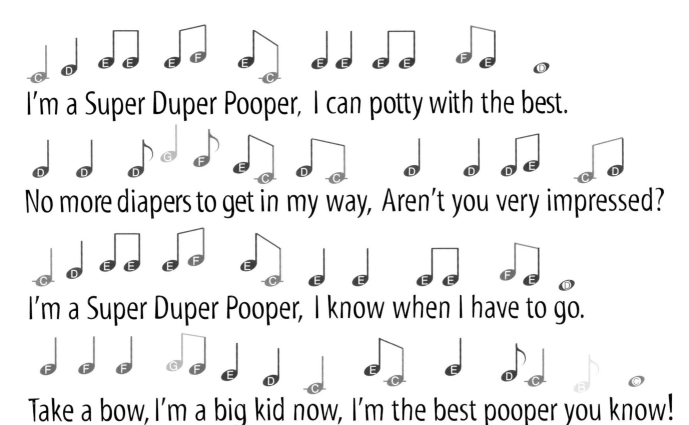

I'm a Super Duper Pooper, I can potty with the best.

No more diapers to get in my way, Aren't you very impressed?

I'm a Super Duper Pooper, I know when I have to go.

Take a bow, I'm a big kid now, I'm the best pooper you know!

Yeahhhhhhh, Lizzie!

Come on, let's go!
The party's about to begin!
Let's hurry or we'll miss the
Polka Dot Clown."

I'M A CLOWN
I'M A CLOWN

I try to make you laugh

Don't like to see you frown.

I'M A CLOWN I'M A CLOWN

I want to make you smile when you are feeling down.

We'll make magic— you have it up your sleeve.

We'll make magic, if you just believe.

I'M A CLOWN

So are YOU.

Put on your party smile!

You'll be a great

CLOWN too!

While watching the Polka Dot Clown,
Bobby began to **WRIGGLE.**
Then he *JIGGLED.*
Bobby just couldn't sit still!

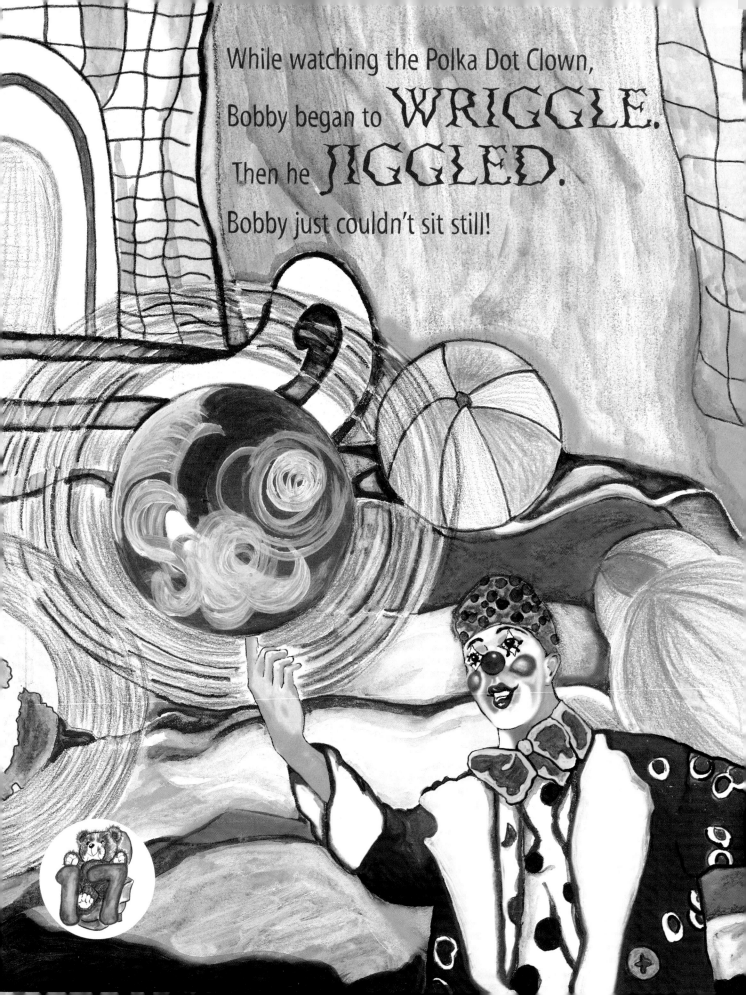

Then his magical friend, Mr. Penders, said, "Listen Bobby, I'm going to tell you something most important" he whispered…

"It can happen when you're sitting very quietly,
It can happen when you're standing
there under a tree.
It could happen to a he,
It could happen to a she,
But, you'll always know
When you have to pee!"

I need to go to the potty," said Bobby.
"Me too!" said Zachary.
"Me too," said Jonathan.
Lizzie said, "I already
went to the potty."

18

19

Bobby rushes to the potty first.
He remembers to lift the toilet seat.
Then he begins to sing…

SUNG TO THE TUNE OF *TRA LA LA BOOM DE AY*

Tra-la-la-boom-de-ay…
I push my pants away,
And while I'm standing there,
Pull down my underwear.

Tra-la-la-boom-de-ay.
No diapers in the way.
Now I wear underwear,
Don't need a potty chair.

When Bobby's finished, he puts the lid back down
and gets ready to return to the party.

But Mr. Penders calls him back.

"Hey sport, don't be in a rush. Did you forget?
You always have to flush!"

"One more step there buckaroo!
Wash up like Mommy told you to."

This is the way I pull up my sleeves,
pull up my sleeves, pull up my sleeves.
This is the way I turn on the tap
right after I go to the potty."

This is the way we soap our hands,
soap our hands, soap our hands.
This is the way we soap our hands
right after we go to the potty."

This is the way we rinse them off,
rinse them off, rinse them off.
This is the way we rinse them off,
right after we go to the potty!

This is the way we wipe our hands,
wipe our hands, wipe our hands.
This is the way we wipe our hands,
right after we go to the potty.

Pure & Simple SOAP

22

Bobby finished washing up and went back to his party.
What a good time he had with all his friends.

He THANKED his Mom and Dad for the BEST PARTY EVER.

Today was Bobby's birthday, now he is four,
He is growing up now, more and more.
    He can dress himself, he can comb his hair.
He can throw a ball high into the air.

This was Bobby's birthday, we had a cake.
It's a cake that Bobby helped me make.
    From a box of candles, we counted out four,
Each year, Bobby learns more numbers than before.

Now Bobby knows animals by their names,
And he loves to play a hide-and-seek game.
    He can ride a trike, he can sing a song.
And he's old enough to stay up all day long.

This was Bobby's birthday, and he is four, And he just keeps learning more and more.

It is with pride that
Katy now sings…
"I use my potty
when I have to pee."

Lizzie joyfully announces…
"I'm a Super Duper Pooper,
I'm the best pooper you know!"

She teaches her Teddy to…
"Wipe, wipe, wipe yourself,
always front to back."

And Bobby will never forget Mr. Penders' lessons… "Lift the toilet seat and put it back down… Don't forget! You always have to flush!"

And… "Wash up like Mommy told you to!"

So now, Katy, Lizzie and Bobby, by being the greatest SUPER DUPER POOPERS, bring a happy ending to the story **"It's Potty Time."**

Super Duper Pooper!

LEARNING™
Through Entertainment, Inc.

THE COMPANY THAT BROUGHT YOU
THE VERY SUCCESSFUL VIDEO
IT'S POTTY TIME™
OF THE DUKE FAMILY SERIES INTRODUCES
3 NEW PRODUCTS!

You can watch it anytime on your t.v...

AWARD WINNING VIDEO
Proven effective...makes toilet training fun!
It's Potty Time™ shows all the steps of using the
bathroom in a delightful way, children love to
watch again and again. Before you know it, your
child will be saying, "I did it all by myself."

THE DUKE FAMILY SERIES
Approved By The Duke University Medical Center

VIDEO

You can read it sitting on your grandma's knee...

BOOK

NEW!
IT'S POTTY TIME™ BOOK
Beautifully illustrated, entertaining, and
a good learning tool for children.
Teaches them the basic skills to become
Super Duper Poopers.

AUDIO CASSETTE

You can listen to it underneath a tree!

NEW!
It's Potty Time™ Audio Cassette
Soundtrack of the award-winning
video containing the hit song
"SUPER DUPER POOPER"
by Loonis McGlohon.

AUDIO CASSETTE

NEW!
MELODIES AND
LULLABIES™
AUDIO CASSETTE
TAPE!
Melodies and Lullabies™
let children drift gently off
to sleep. Original music by
Loonis McGlohon.

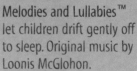

To receive 6 **Super Duper Pooper!** stickers, call 1-800-23 POTTY
1-800-237-6889